21 DAYS

PRAYER • MEDITATION • APPLICATION

TONYA N. ANDERSON, M. MIN

DEDICATION

I dedicate this book to everyone who understands prayer as a vital component of spiritual warfare and warriors who have and continue to avail their lives to the ministry of deliverance.

Special thanks to the members of Abundant Life Ministries Family Worship Center for supporting and encouraging your First Lady.

To my mother, Wilhelmina Nixon *(affectionately called Ms. Peggy)*, who exemplified the value of diligence and perseverance while beating the odds of a single mother raising four children; three sons and her only daughter, me. To my maternal grandmother, Lila Mae King, who's prayer mantle taught me how to be strategic in warfare. I am convinced that the praying legacy has been transferred and now rest on me.

This book is also dedicated to my husband, Kenneth A. Anderson, who continues to be a great support of what God is doing in my life. To my three children, Kristle, Kristopher, and Katrina; you all play a vital part in my ability to boldly declare freedom in the lives of people everywhere. I'm honored to be called, "Nana" by my grandson Kendrick and granddaughter Londyn; Nana loves you!

Thank you Lord for all my many blessings!

FOREWORD

Priority, as an adjective, is defined as *highest or higher in importance, rank, or privilege*. In our society, we are inundated with hectic schedules. It appears that 24 hours is not enough time. How can we add a few more to our day? We sleep less, eat on the run, interact via social media and still barely accomplish our tasks. We are extremely busy; so busy that we hardly have time for God.

Our world is being challenged on many fronts. Racism, terrorism, financial struggles, political concerns, just to name a few. It is imperative that we as a society constantly seek the LORD! 2 Chronicles 7:14 lets us know, if we seek God, He will intercede and bring change to our world. Intercede means to interrupt. What the above scripture implies is that God will interrupt what has been planned and turn it around for the good. No matter how busy we get, we can never get too busy to where we deprive ourselves of some alone time with God. There are many benefits to spending time in the presence of our all-mighty God. Peace, joy, calm and stability are just a few of the benefits received while being in His presence.

It is widely understood that if you spend 21 days doing something it becomes a habit. If you make your fitness your top priority, then after 21 consecutive days exercising becomes second nature. When it comes to starting and continuing a daily devotional schedule, many have no idea where to start. As in exercising & dieting, most people start with an established work-out and meal plan. So, I present to you the 21 Daily Devotion presented by my lovely wife, Tonya N. Anderson.

There is no limit to the level of spiritual strength, empowerment, growth and insight you will acquire by scheduling and participating in this daily journey into the presence of the LORD. Tonya has been moved by God to share with you from her personal experiences of seeking the face of God on a daily basis. So just as you would follow the diet to the letter, follow this "Daily Devotion" to increase your place in God.

Tonya speaks to and hears from God on a daily basis. Through the challenges of life, it has always been her determination to find that alone time with the LORD. It is in these quiet times that she can discern what the Lord requires and what He wants to convey to His people. I encourage you to take this journey along with her. I am confident that as you use this devotional as a guide to establish your personal plan to seek God, your spiritual stamina will increase and your communication with the All Mighty will become stronger. Make your daily devotion your *"Top Priority!"*

Kenneth A. Anderson

CONTENT

21
DAYS

PRAYER • MEDITATION • APPLICATION

INTRODUCTION

I have come to believe that we all have the right to a prosperous and victorious life in every situation. Anything other than this we would be a mockery to God.

Well, the devil thought he had me but I prevailed. The warrior in me stood the test of time. I had to decide rather I wanted my life to be filled with repetitive chaos or constant freedom.

This book is birthed from a place called "A Warrior's Life". It's an experience of countless intimate times in the presence of the Lord. Periodically, God would drop little nuggets in my spirit called, "words of wisdom". This wisdom produced inspiring quotes to assure me that I was not alone in the many battles and spiritual warfare I encountered.

Life situations will divinely produce powerful, encouraging, and motivating quotes! Applied knowledge produces the ability to live life without regrets knowing that God has placed a champion inside of you.

This book allows me to share a few moments in life where I had to make tough decisions. Would I fold under pressure or respond through prayer and application of God's Word? My experience is worth rehearsing because I believe every battle I endured will help others overcome intense moments of fatigue, frustration, and discouragement. It's my prayer that this 21-day journey will have a lasting impact on your life.

Understanding the discipline of prayer, meditation, and application has afforded me the grace to live a humble but bold, purposed-filled life. Religion did not get me here; rather, an authentic relationship with Christ. I'm free to laugh, dance, and simply free to be me!

As you read and incorporate the spiritual and natural principles presented in this book, I trust the warrior in you will come alive. Remember, daily devotion will cause you to stand against any and all forces of the enemy.

Day 1
Time brings Opportunity

PRAYER

Heavenly Father, I thank you that today's opportunity will bring about tomorrow's productivity for my life. Thank you Lord for not withholding anything you have planned for me. I declare that the plans you have for my life will come unhindered and unchecked by any demonic force. I declare that today is a fresh start for me. I announce that I will overcome every obstacle, move past every defeating moment, and come through every challenge better than I was before. Amen. *(Jeremiah1:5; Philippians 4:13)*

MEDITATION

Isaiah 55:10-11 (NIV) - The rain and snow come down from the heavens and stay on the ground to water the earth. They cause the grain to grow, producing seed for the farmer and bread for the hungry. It is the same with my word. I send it out, and it always produces fruit. It will accomplish all I want it to, and it will prosper everywhere I send it.

Genesis 8:22 (NIV) - As long as the earth remains, there will be planting and harvest, cold and heat, summer and winter, day, and night.

APPLICATION

The importance of having patience is to have the ability not to rush to accomplish a plan that may not be the will of God for your life. Remember, time offers the opportunity to think about what's best and what your desired outcome should look like. Be careful not to minimize the waiting period nor the time it takes to get there; you may just have to start over. With time, things will get better. All the right people will come to your aid and ultimately your goals will be accomplished. With time, comes another opportunity to either do something a different way or do something that fits you better than what you may have tried before.

James 1:4 paints the picture perfectly, "Let perseverance finish its work so that you may be mature and complete, not lacking anything" (NIV).

Journal of Daily Reflections

Day 2

Something Different cost more than Something Simple

PRAYER

Heavenly Father, I thank you for making me unique and extraordinary. Thank you for shaping me into the image of your dear Son Jesus Christ. Because of You, I can "run through troops and leap over walls" *(Ps. 18:29)*. Thank you Lord for creating me to do great and mighty things. Thank you Lord for your craftsmanship of me is marvelous. You thought of me even before I was formed in my mother's womb. I declare that I can do all things through Christ Jesus. Amen

MEDITATION

Matthew 3:1-4 (NIV) - In those days John the Baptist came, preaching in the wilderness of Judea and saying, Repent, for the kingdom of heaven has come near. This is he who was spoken of through the prophet Isaiah: A voice of one calling in the wilderness, 'Prepare the way for the Lord, make straight paths for him. John's clothes were made of camel's hair, and he had a leather belt around his waist. His food was locusts and wild honey.

Romans 12:4-8 (NIV) - For just as each of us has one body with many members, and these members do not all have the same function, so in Christ we, though many, form one body, and each member belongs to all the others. We have different gifts, according to the grace given to each of us. If your gift is prophesying, then prophesy in accordance with your faith; if it is serving, then serve; if it is teaching, then teach; if it is to encourage, then give encouragement; if it is giving, then give generously; if it is to lead, do it diligently; if it is to show mercy, do it cheerfully.

APPLICATION

I have come to realize that everything in life is not easy. If it's worth having, you will be required to courageously move toward obtaining what you want along this journey. Furthermore, it will require enduring strength. It takes less effort to quit, than it does to keep going. Stop waiting for someone to make the way easy for you.

John the Baptist dressed different, had an unusual diet and perhaps was just an all-around different kind of guy. Nevertheless, he still carried out his God given assignment. The cost of being different is an expensive price to pay but yields great dividends.

Journal of Daily Reflections

_____

_____

_____

_____

_____

_____

_____

_____

_____

_____

_____

_____

_____

_____

_____

_____

_____

_____

_____

_____

_____

_____

_____

_____

Day 3
Your Destiny is Connected to How you Think

PRAYER

Heavenly Father, I have come to realize that because of you I can do great and mighty things. Thank you for being my road-map to success. Because of you I can do all things by your strength. I boldly confess that fear is not a part of my life; therefore, I renounce any and all forms of debilitating and tormenting thoughts in my mind. I put my trust in you oh Lord; I abandon the idea of giving up. I will operate in confidence in every area of my life at full throttle. Thank you Lord for never leaving me hopeless nor forsaking me to defend for myself. Amen. *(Phil. 4:13; Hebrews 13:5)*

MEDITATION

Proverbs 4:23 (NIV) - Above all else, guard your heart, for everything you do flows from it. Keep your mouth free of perversity; keep corrupt talk far from your lips. Let your eyes look straight ahead; fix your gaze directly before you. Give careful thought to the paths for your feet and be steadfast in all your ways. Do not turn to the right or the left; keep your foot from evil.

Ps. 138:8 (NIV) - The LORD will vindicate me; your love, LORD, endures forever—do not abandon the works of your hands.

Eph. 6:10-12 (NIV) - Finally, be strong in the Lord and in his mighty power. Put on the full armor of God, so that you can take your stand against the devil's schemes. For our struggle is not against flesh and blood, but against the rulers, against the authorities, against the powers of this dark world and against the spiritual forces of evil in the heavenly realms.

Numbers 13:30 (NIV) - Then Caleb silenced the people before Moses and said, "We should go up and take possession of the land, for we can certainly do it."

APPLICATION

The more you think about a thing the more it will likely become your reality. Favor yourself with a mind of a champion. The way to do this is to never underestimate the giant in you. Give yourself permission to dismiss such lies spoken to you throughout your life, "you are worthless — you will never amount to anything." Begin to employ God's truth which affirms that you are "fearfully and wonderfully made" (Psalm 139:14). You have a right to access God's promises made to you! Therefore, you must think positive and speak positive in order to experience God's blessings predetermined for you.

Journal of Daily Reflections

_____

_____

_____

_____

_____

_____

_____

_____

_____

_____

_____

_____

_____

_____

_____

_____

_____

_____

_____

_____

_____

_____

_____

_____

Day 4
What you say Guides
you to your Final Destination

PRAYER

Heavenly Father, I thank you that with every step I take, You are there to carry me the next step further. I declare that there's nothing beyond my ability to achieve. I have what it takes to be the best at whatever I strive to do. I am the head and not the tail. I'm blessed when I come in and go out. I am diligent; I am vigilant; and I press toward my highest goals without looking back. My past will not interfere with my present or future. I am more than confident that you are with me. In Jesus' Name, Amen.

MEDITATION

Philippians 4:13 (KJV) - I can do all things through Christ who strengthens me.

Proverbs 3:5-6 (KJV) - Trust in the LORD with all your heart; and lean not on your own understanding. In all your ways acknowledge him, and he shall direct your paths.

Proverbs 18:20-21 (KJV) - A man's belly shall be satisfied with the fruit of his mouth; and with the increase of his lips shall he be filled. Death and life are in the power of the tongue: and they that love it shall eat the fruit thereof.

Proverbs 19:20-21 (KJV) - Hear counsel, and receive instruction, that thou mayest be wise in thy latter end. There are many devices in a man's heart; nevertheless the counsel of the Lord, that shall stand.

APPLICATION

As sons and daughters of the Kingdom, be careful how you allow destructive words to shape your life. It's a great risk to take that will inevitably stop you from getting to your expected end. What you say could be the vehicle that takes you to a place of total victory or drive you to ultimate failure.

An old proverbial statement, "He who does not know where he's going will probably end up some place else."

See yourself far better than how the enemy defines you. Release yourself from all forms of intimidation. God didn't bring you into the land of promise with no intent for you to possess it. Adopt the spirit of Caleb and Joshua who saw beyond natural barriers (Numbers 13:27-33). Instead of verbalizing how you fell in the moment, rehearse how you will come out, "I am well able.

Journal of Daily Reflections

_____

_____

_____

_____

_____

_____

_____

_____

_____

_____

_____

_____

_____

_____

_____

_____

_____

_____

_____

_____

_____

_____

_____

_____

Day 5

The enemy never wins

PRAYER

Heavenly Father, thank you for exposing my enemies and helping me realize that you are more for me than the world against me. Thank you for giving me clear vision in order to remain focused, leaping over hurdles, and defeating all obstacles. I hear the voice of the Good Shepherd and a stranger I will not follow. I utilize my keys to the Kingdom to take authority, binding what you have bound in heaven, and shutting down all channels of communication which oppose the plan and purpose God has for my life. Today, I choose not to walk in the counsel of the ungodly, nor sit in the seat of scornful, but to delight myself in God's Word. Amen *(Romans 8:31; Psalms 1:1; Matthew 16:19)*

MEDITATION

Jeremiah 29:11 (ERV) - I say this because I know the plans that I have for you. This message is from the LORD. "I have good plans for you. I don't plan to hurt you. I plan to give you hope and a good future."

Isa. 54:17 (KVJ) - No weapon that is formed against thee shall prosper; and every tongue that shall rise against thee in judgment thou shalt condemn. This is the heritage of the servants of the LORD, and their righteousness is of me, saith the LORD.

3 John 2 (KJV) - Beloved, I wish above all things that thou mayest prosper and be in health, even as thy soul prospereth.

APPLICATION

Recognizing the real enemy helps you not to blame God for misfortune. Satan constantly puts us on trial before God in order to challenge our faith and obedience.

Satan may have dominion in the earth but he doesn't have rule over you! You always WIN through Jesus Christ.

Journal of Daily Reflections

_____

_____

_____

_____

_____

_____

_____

_____

_____

_____

_____

_____

_____

_____

_____

_____

_____

_____

_____

_____

_____

_____

_____

_____

_____

Day 6

Never govern your life based on the opinion of others

PRAYER

Lord, it's me again calling on your righteous and majestic Name. Thank you for thinking so much of me that you chose to create me in your image and likeness. I have come to realize that everything you created was good and has become your prized possession. I am accepted by the Beloved who gives me the grace, gifts, and ability to thrive. Therefore, I commit my works into your hands with great excitement. I am confident that you will prove your plan for me in the earth. I declare that my mind is renewed and my life is confirmed based on God's plan and not man's thoughts. No longer will I follow the mundane blueprint for my life. Rather, I will obey God's good, perfect and acceptable will. Amen.
(Genesis 1:27; 1 Timothy 4:4; Proverbs 16:3; Romans 12:6-7; Romans 12:2)

MEDITATION

1 Samuel 16:7 (ESV) "But the LORD said to Samuel, "Do not look on his appearance or on the height of his stature, because I have rejected him. For the LORD sees not as man sees: man looks on the outward appearance, but the LORD looks on the heart."

Psalms 139: 14-16 (ESV) "I praise you, for I am fearfully and wonderfully made. Wonderful are your works; my soul knows it very well. My frame was not hidden from you, when I was being made in secret, intricately woven in the depths of the earth. Your eyes saw my unformed substance; in your book were written, every one of them, the days that were formed for me, when as yet there was none of them."

1 Corinthians 15:10 (ESV) "But by the grace of God I am what I am, and his grace toward me was not in vain. On the contrary, I worked harder than any of them, though it was not I, but the grace of God that is with me."

APPLICATION

Do you ever get annoyed by how others seem to know what's best for you? Well, you can control just how much power you yield to those who have a personal view of how you should govern your life. If you are not careful that same person will persuade you to model who they are, forfeiting who you are destined to become. Don't be guilty of "cloning".

Do you remember as a child when someone would copy everything you did and how irritating that was?

You would say to that person, "stop copying me". Take pride in being an original and not a copy. Be proud and unashamed of who God has created you to be. We are not all called to do the same nor be the same.

Be careful of wasting a lifetime trying to measure up to unrealistic expectations. Know that you are God's original masterpiece.

Journal of Daily Reflections

Day 7
Weed out anything that Hinders or Stops your Garden from Growing

PRAYER

Heavenly Father thank you for being my strength and my redeemer. You, Oh God causes me to rest in the meadows grass and lead me beside the calming streams. Lord, I am captivated by your love for me and desire for me to have the best. Thank you for showing me the way I should take. Thank you for helping me see more of what I need rather than what I want. Your guidance gives me the ability to discern good and evil. I acknowledge that I can do nothing apart from you. Lord, I welcome you into my life; cultivate new growth so that I can bear much fruit. In Jesus' Name. Amen *(Psalm 23: 2; John 15:5)*

MEDITATION

Galatians 5:1 (NIV) - It is for freedom that Christ has set us free. Stand firm, then, and do not let yourselves be burdened again by a yoke of slavery.

Isa. 58:11 (NIV) - The Lord will guide you always; he will satisfy your needs in a sun-scorched land and will strengthen your frame. You will be like a well-watered garden, like a spring whose waters never fail.

Psalm 1:3 (NIV) - That person is like a tree planted by streams of water, which yields its fruit in season and whose leaf does not wither—whatever they do prospers.

APPLICATION

It is the will of God that we operate at maximum capacity spiritually. Spiritual pruning takes place when God removes sin and worldly distractions in order for us to bear fruit. There are two types of pruning: one is cutting off and the other is cutting back. There are some people, places and things you must cut off. Then there are times you may just have to pull back from; in other words known as "trimming".

Pruning is the process of getting rid of things that are undesirable and/or clearing the way for a much healthier growth.

Beware of the python spirit, which easily creeps in with the purpose of squeezing the life out of you causing you to disconnect from God. Its purpose is to deprive you of the necessary air you breathe. Avoid people and places that have potential to detour you spiritually and naturally. I encourage you to gather your garden tools *(prayer and the Word of God);* use them to weed out all destructive devices of the enemy.

Journal of Daily Reflections

_____

_____

_____

_____

_____

_____

_____

_____

_____

_____

_____

_____

_____

_____

_____

_____

_____

_____

_____

_____

_____

_____

_____

_____

_____

Day 8

Faith or Foolishness

PRAYER

Heavenly Father, thank you for opening my eyes to the truth of your Word which informs that when I pray believe, receive, and I shall have it. I also understand that if I pray improperly I will not receive. Lord, as I draw close to thee knowing that you are always there, I trust that you will reward me greatly with your presence. As I turn toward you, I'm turning away from what seems wise in my eyes. I declare that I will only follow wise counsel in order to avoid falling far from you Oh Lord. Amen. *(Mark 11:24; James 4:3; Hebrews 11:6; Luke 6:39)*

MEDITATION

Hebrews 11:5,7-9, 11 (KJV) - By faith Abel offered unto God a more excellent sacrifice than Cain, by which he obtained witness that he was righteous, God testifying of his gifts: and by it he being dead yet speaketh. **By faith** Noah, being warned of God of things not seen as yet, moved with fear, prepared an ark to the saving of his house; by the which he condemned the world, and became heir of the righteousness which is by faith. **By faith** Abraham, when he was called to go out into a place which he should after receive for an inheritance, obeyed; and he went out, not knowing whither he went. **By faith** he sojourned in the land of promise, as in a strange country, dwelling in tabernacles with Isaac and Jacob, the heirs with him of the same promise: **Through faith** also Sara herself received strength to conceive seed, and was delivered of a child when she was past age, because she judged him faithful who had promised.

APPLICATION

If God said it and instructed you to do it, believe that it will come to pass. God will never tell you something or instruct you to do something that He is not willing to make good on or bring to pass in your life.

It's foolish when we step out on our own and expect God to act on our behalf. It's like praying for a house when it's already occupied. It's like praying for that one spouse and they belong to someone else. That's foolish!

Faith aligns itself with the Will of God, the Word of God, and the promise of God. Another way of looking at Faith is knowing that "even if God doesn't do it, He is still able." Faith is not waving a magic wand and asking God to make your wish come true. Faith is trusting that God knows best and He never fails. Be assured of this one thing, if God said *it*, believe *it* and patiently wait for the manifestation.

Journal of Daily Reflections

Day 9

Faith says *"no"* to what it looks like now and *"yes"* to what it has the potential to become

PRAYER

Dear Heavenly Father, I acknowledge prayer to be a vital part of my spiritual life knowing that if I diligently seek you, rewards await me. Lord, you never cease to amaze me. I give you all the glory for the mighty works you are doing in and through my life. Thank you for doing far more than what I could ever imagine. Today, I yield myself to believe in spite of how I feel. I continue to learn how to obey and trust you, even when I don't have a full picture of where you are directing me. Assuredly, the promises made to me will be fulfilled in the earth. Amen. (*Hebrew 11:6, Ephesians 3:20*)

MEDITATION

Ezekiel 16:1-14 (NIV) - The word of the LORD came to me: "Son of man, confront Jerusalem with her detestable practices and say, 'This is what the Sovereign LORD says to Jerusalem: Your ancestry and birth were in the land of the Canaanites; your father was an Amorite and your mother a Hittite. On the day you were born your cord was not cut, nor were you washed with water to make you clean, nor were you rubbed with salt or wrapped in cloths. No one looked on you with pity or had compassion enough to do any of these things for you. Rather, you were thrown out into the open field, for on the day you were born you were despised. **'Then I passed by and saw you kicking about in your blood, and as you lay there in your blood I said to you, "Live!"** I made you grow like a plant of the field. You grew and developed and entered puberty. Your breasts had formed and your hair had grown, yet you were stark naked. Later I passed by, and when I looked at you and saw that you were old enough for love, I spread the corner of my garment over you and covered your naked body. I gave you my solemn oath and entered into a covenant with you, declares the Sovereign LORD, and you became mine. I bathed you with water and washed the blood from you and put ointments on you. I clothed you with an embroidered dress and put sandals of fine leather on you. I dressed you in fine linen and covered you with costly garments. I adorned you with jewelry: I put bracelets on your arms and a necklace around your neck, and I put a ring on your nose, earrings on your ears and a beautiful crown on your head. So you were adorned with gold and silver; your clothes were of fine linen and costly fabric and embroidered cloth. Your food was honey, olive oil and the finest flour. You became very beautiful and rose to be a queen. And your fame spread among the nations on account of your beauty, because the splendor I had given you made your beauty perfect, declares the Sovereign LORD.

Philippians 1:6 (NIV) - Being confident of this, that he who began a good work in you will carry it on to completion until the day of Christ Jesus.

APPLICATION

There are times when we pray about a situation and instead of getting better, things get worse. This causes our heart to grow weary and perhaps lose faith. You are not alone. During these challenging times in my life I would talk to the Lord, "God, whatever you're doing in this season of my life, I make a concretive effort to stand on your promises and trust you for the best outcome." Being a man or woman of faith, giving up is never an option.

Never consult your past regarding your future because it (meaning your past) has a way of deceiving you!

Journal of Daily Reflections

Day 10

Don't just read God's Word
but experience God's Word

PRAYER

Oh God, I am so grateful that you are always with us and promised never to leave or forsake us. What a delight to know that in the beginning you became flesh and dwelt among us. I find great pleasure in mediating on your Word. I am grateful that your Word is active in my life to judge the intent of my heart. Thank you for leading me into righteousness for your name sake. Your Word guides, protects, shields, and directs me. Your Word has given me authority to rule and reign over all powers of the enemy. I declare my life as a tree planted by the rivers of water bringing forth much fruit. In Jesus' name, Amen.
(John 1:1, Deuteronomy 31:8, Hebrew 4:12, Psalm 23:3, Psalm 1:5)

MEDIATION

Psalm 34:8 (KJV) - O taste and see that the LORD is good: blessed is the man that trusteth in him.

Job 42:5 (KJV) - I have heard of thee by the hearing of the ear: but now mine eye seeth thee.

1 Corinthians 2:9-10 (KJV) - But as it is written, Eye hath not seen, nor ear heard, neither have entered into the heart of man, the things which God hath prepared for them that love him. But God hath revealed them unto us by his Spirit: for the Spirit searcheth all things, yea, the deep things of God.

APPLICATION

God's Word is special and should be handled with much care. The Word applied yields an extraordinary experience that leaves a lasting impact. The Word is like an animated picture show. I love how it comes alive in our lives.

The Word hid in your heart helps to push you far away from the temptation of sin. The Word brings much freedom and deliverance. See it, read it, and apply it.

I prophecy truth to you today, "There's a new dimension in God you must experience. God desires to stretch you to your maximum potential. His plan is to make you larger than you have ever been!"

Journal of Daily Reflections

Day 11
The Power of the Spoken Word

PRAYER

Dear God, today I exercise my authority in the earth and speak the Word of Faith over my life. I declare that I'm prospering in the things of God. My body is healed. I'm spirit-filled. I walk in divide favor. No one can resist helping me as I walk out the fulfilment of God's purpose for my life. I am full of love and loved by all. I boldly confess my life will never be the same in Jesus Name, Amen.

MEDIATION

Proverbs 18:21 (NIV) - The tongue has the power of life and death, and those who love it will eat its fruit.

Psalms 33:6 (KJV) - By the word of the LORD were the heavens made; and all the host of them by the breath of his mouth.

James 3:8-10 (NIV) - But no human being can tame the tongue. It is a restless evil, full of

deadly poison. With the tongue we praise our Lord and Father, and with it we curse human beings, who have been made in God's likeness. Out of the same mouth come praise and cursing. My brothers and sisters, this should not be.

Matthew 24:35 (NIV) - Heaven and earth will pass away, but my words will never pass away.

Numbers 23:19 (NIV) - God is not human, that he should lie, not a human being, that he should change his mind. Does he speak and then not act? Does he promise and not fulfill?

APPLICATION

The world was framed by the words God spoke. This principle applies to us. What we say breathes life or death. If you don't want to experience negativity, you shouldn't speak negative. More than less, what we tend to speak out of our mouth has already taken root in our heart.

When we change what we say, we change the reality of our world. There is a realm in which God has prepared for us, but we must say what God says.

Journal of Daily Reflections

_____

_____

_____

_____

_____

_____

_____

_____

_____

_____

_____

_____

_____

_____

_____

_____

_____

_____

_____

_____

_____

_____

_____

_____

_____

_____

Day 12
Project a Better End for Yourself

PRAYER

Heavenly Father, I pronounce the failure of the enemy's plan to stop me from experiencing prosperity and hope in Jesus Christ. Thank you for allowing the Holy Spirit to intercept and block every fiery dart of the enemy. Thank you for revealing the plans that you have for me which overrule every plan the enemy meant to bring harm. I will arrive to the expected end you have for my life. In Jesus Name, Amen. *(Jeremiah 29:11)*

MEDITATION

Psalm 22:19 (NIV) - But you, LORD, do not be far from me. You are my strength; come quickly to help me.

Psalm 28:7-8 (NIV) - The LORD is my strength and my shield; my heart trusts in him, and he helps me. My heart leaps for joy, and with my song I praise him. The LORD is the strength of his people, a fortress of salvation for his anointed one.

Isaiah 40:31 (NIV) - but those who hope in the LORD will renew their strength. They will soar on wings like eagles; they will run and not grow weary, they will walk and not be faint.

2 Corinthians 12:9-10 (NIV) - But he said to me, "My grace is sufficient for you, for my power is made perfect in weakness." Therefore I will boast all the more gladly about my weaknesses, so that Christ's power may rest on me. That is why, for Christ's sake, I delight in weaknesses, in insults, in hardships, in persecutions, in difficulties. For when I am weak, then I am strong.

APPLICATION

Do you have recurring temptations that you find difficult to resist? Although the Bible makes it very clear that we have won the victory over Satan and his evil kingdom through Jesus Christ, there is still a war waging to conquer our souls.

Begin to purge yourself from anything that stimulates worldly lust. Your life is intended to glorify God. Remain alert of tactics the enemy employs to gain unauthorized access to your life, property and possessions.

See yourself in the future living better than you do right now. You must have vision to project a better end for yourself.

Journal of Daily Reflections

Day 13

When wrong people leave your life, right things start to happen

PRAYER

Dear Heavenly Father, thank you for helping me discern good and evil. Thank you for teaching my hands to war and giving my fingers skill for battle. Lord, you continue to open my eyes to know when I'm dealing with an enemy whose main purpose is to stop me from reaching my ultimate goal. Thank you for showing me that what had become familiar to me was actually hindering me from living in the land of plenty. You continue to lead me in a path that leads to righteousness. I see myself walking through doors that no man can shut. Today, I declare restoration for the years the devourer has taken from me. In Jesus Name, Amen. *(Psalm 144:1; Genesis 12:1; Psalm 23:3; Joel 2:25)*

MEDITATION

Proverbs 13:20 (KJV) - He who walks with wise men will be wise, But the companion of fools will suffer harm.

Proverbs 14:7 (KJV) - Go from the presence of a foolish man, when thou perceivest not in him the lips of knowledge.

Job 22:28 (KJV) - Thou shalt also decree a thing, and it shall be established unto thee: and the light shall shine upon thy ways.

2 Corinthians 9:8 (KJV) - And God is able to make all grace abound toward you; that ye, always having all sufficiency in all things, may abound to every good work.

Ephesians 3:20 (KJV) - Now unto him that is able to do exceeding abundantly above all that we ask or think, according to the power that worketh in us.

APPLICATION

I've encountered individuals who appear to have an addiction to chaos. Their daily confessions were filled with negative overtones. They seem to find the worse even in the good. It was rare that you heard anything positive come out of their mouth.

The bible shares a great example of what happens when you surround yourself and connect with the wrong people: "Don't be fooled: Bad friends will ruin good habits" - I Corinthians 15:33.

Too often do we hold on to things that will inevitably depreciate in value as opposed to holding on to things that will add value to our relationship with God. Don't allow your relationship with unbelievers to separate you from the sure and firm relationship you have established in Christ Jesus.

Everything that comes in your life is not intended to have permanent residency. Learn to accept the idea of eliminating all the wrong people from your scope of influence.

Waiting for you are opportunities that will catapult you to greater dimensions. Be confident knowing that immeasurable increase is knocking at your door.

Journal of Daily Reflections

_____

_____

_____

_____

_____

_____

_____

_____

_____

_____

_____

_____

_____

_____

_____

_____

_____

_____

_____

_____

_____

_____

_____

Day 14

Operate on the level God graced you with

PRAYER

Oh Lord, Our God, how excellent is thy name in all the earth. God, you showed forth my worth and value in that you made me only a little lower than the angels and yourself. Lord you trusted me with tremendous authority and responsibility in the earth. For this I give you praise and honor. Thank you for all you have done. I stand to give you glory acknowledging that you are God above the heavens and you reign above the earth. I magnify your name. Yes, I magnify Your Name. *(Psalm 8:1,5-6)*

MEDITATION

Philippians 2:13 (KJV) - For it is God which worketh in you both to will and to do of his good pleasure.

Ephesians 2:10 (KJV) - For we are his workmanship, created in Christ Jesus unto good works, which God hath before ordained that we should walk in them.

Psalm 90:17 (KJV) - And let the beauty of the Lord our God be upon us: and establish thou the work of our hands upon us; yea, the work of our hands establish thou it.

Hebrews 13:21 (KJV) -Make you perfect in every good work to do his will, working in you that which is well pleasing in his sight, through Jesus Christ; to whom be glory for ever and ever. Amen

APPLICATION

God created us to bring Him glory. He wants us to operate in our authentic and unique calling.

Be careful not to serve in an area that produces busyness rather than productivity. I often observe individuals comparing their area of ministry to what they see others doing. It's like putting a size 12 inch foot in a size 7 shoe......"ouch!" God doesn't always give you what you want but He will give you what you can handle.

Have peace with the level of responsibility God has graced you with; it fits you: **Philippians 1:6 (NLT),** "And I am certain that God, who began the good work within you, will continue his work until it is finally finished on the day when Christ Jesus returns."

What's about to take place in your life cannot be measured by human hands but it's established through the power and the mighty hand of God. Nothing and no one will be able to stop what God is doing in your life: **Ephesians 6:11 (NLT)**, "Put on all of God's armor so that you will be able to stand firm against all strategies of the devil".

Journal of Daily Reflections

Day 15
What's in your hand?

PRAYER

Oh Lord, my God, I'm in awe of the wonderful things you are about to do through the works of my hands. I take great pleasure and yield myself to you. Lord, you thought enough of me to place me in the ministry. Therefore, I strive not to neglect the gift you placed in me. As a sign of true worship, I present my body to you as a living sacrifice; holy and well-pleasing to you. In Jesus Name, Amen. *(1 Timothy 1:12; Acts 19:11; Romans 12:1])*

MEDITATION

Psalm 90:17 (NLT) - And may the Lord our God show us his approval and make our efforts successful. Yes, make our efforts successful!"

Isaiah 41:10 (NLT) - Don't be afraid, for I am with you. Don't be discouraged, for I am your God. I will strengthen you and help you. I will hold you up with my victorious right hand.

Psalm 150:1-6 (NLT) - Praise the LORD! Praise God in his sanctuary; praise him in his mighty heaven! Praise him for his mighty works; praise his unequaled greatness! Praise him with a blast of the ram's horn; praise him with the lyre and harp! Praise him with the tambourine and dancing; praise him with strings and flutes! Praise him with a clash of cymbals; praise him with loud clanging cymbals. Let everything that breathes sing praises to the LORD! Praise the LORD!"

APPLICATION

As I talked with my cousin Beverly Scruggs (*BJ*), we both shared how God is not limited by our natural born deficiency. Rather, He sees great potential and possibility.

After God's extended conversation with Moses and hearing how much he lacked in his ability to lead Israel, God asked Moses this question, "What's in your hand" (Exodus 4:2).

Why wait for someone's approval when God approves you? Use what's in your hand.

Journal of Daily Reflections

Day 16
Carry the Torch

PRAYER

Oh Lord, my God, before you formed me in my mother's womb, you ordained me to minister life to a dying world. You created me to announce freedom to those who are bound and demonically oppressed. Lord, you have given me authority over all the powers of the enemy. I declare that I will not be shaken, moved, harmed, or fearful of any attacks that come at me during the day or the night. Thank you Lord for assigning angels to war on my behalf. Lord, I stand assured of this one thing, that the good work you started in me will be completed. In Jesus Name, Amen. *(Jeremiah 1:5; Luke 4:18; Luke 10:19; Psalm 91:5,11; Philippians 1:6)*

MEDITATION

Matthew 5:14-16 (KJV) - Ye are the light of the world. A city that is set on an hill cannot be hid. Neither do men light a candle, and put it under a bushel, but on a candlestick; and it giveth light unto all that are in the house. "Let your light so shine before men, that they may see your good works, and glorify your Father which is in heaven.

Philippians 2:15 (KJV) - That ye may be blameless and harmless, the sons of God, without rebuke, in the midst of a crooked and perverse nation, among whom ye shine as lights in the world.

APPLICATION

We have a responsibility as representatives of the Kingdom. We have a mandate to model Christ in the earth. God is calling the believer to show the world what the ideal church looks like. Can we confidently instruct others to follow us as we follow Christ? (1 Cor. 11:1)

Carrying the torch requires great strength, commitment, and endurance. Refuse to buckle under the pressure of criticism and those who wrongly ridicule your faith. These are likely the individuals who silently admire you. Stay true to your conviction.

Journal of Daily Reflections

_____

_____

_____

_____

_____

_____

_____

_____

_____

_____

_____

_____

_____

_____

_____

_____

_____

_____

_____

_____

_____

_____

_____

_____

_____

_____

_____

Day 17

Walk through Unexpected Obstacles

PRAYER

Dear God, I am so happy to know that you will never leave me nor forsake me. Even when I can't see or understand what's happening in my life, I'm learning to lean and depend on your love for me. Lord, on the day that I called upon your name, you gave me strength to move forward. Thank you for taking what I lack and adding your supernatural power. Today I am strong and courageous because you oh Lord have gone before me to prepare the way. Amen. (*Psalm 138:3; Deuteronomy 31:6,8*)

MEDITATION

Exodus 13:17-18 (NIV) - When Pharaoh let the people go, God did not lead them on the road through the Philistine country, though that was shorter. For God said, "If they face war, they might change their minds and return to Egypt." So God led the people around by the desert road toward the Red Sea. The Israelites went up out of Egypt ready for battle.

Isaiah 41:17-19 (NIV) - The poor and needy search for water, but there is none; their tongues are parched with thirst. But I the Lord will answer them; I, the God of

Israel, will not forsake them. I will make rivers flow on barren heights, and springs within the valleys. I will turn the desert into pools of water, and the parched ground into springs. I will put in the desert the cedar and the acacia, the myrtle and the olive. I will set junipers in the wasteland, the fir and the cypress together.

Psalm 91:1, 10-16 (KJV) - He that dwelleth in the secret place of the most High shall abide under the shadow of the Almighty. There shall no evil befall thee, neither shall any plague come nigh thy dwelling. For he shall give his angels charge over thee, to keep thee in all thy ways. They shall bear thee up in their hands, lest thou dash thy foot against a stone. Thou shalt tread upon the lion and adder: the young lion and the dragon shalt thou trample under feet. Because he hath set his love upon me, therefore will I deliver him: I will set him on high, because he hath known my name. He shall call upon me, and I will answer him: I will be with him in trouble; I will deliver him, and honour him. With long life will I satisfy him, and shew him my salvation.

APPLICATION

Do you travel to a certain destination using the same route? Imagine how you feel when, without notice, you encounter a road block detailed by a sign that reads, "detour". This could be frustrating, annoying and in some cases scary. All types of emotions grip your heart. The idea of turning around and going back to where you started seem to make better sense in that moment.

Note that all detours are not bad. Some are created to help us avoid impeding danger ahead. Once you've been rerouted, you may begin to see different things that you otherwise would not have experienced if you remained on the familiar route.

Difficult situations are opportunities for your faith to prove genuine and grow stronger in God. The Holy Spirit will enable you to arrive at your intended destination, at the appointed time, fulfilling your intended purpose.

Journal of Daily Reflections

Day 18

Focus

PRAYER

Dear God, today I have decided to lay aside every sin, anxiety, fear, and worry that seeks to trap me. I commit to run this race with endurance having my eyes focused on you. Lord, I look to you as my example. You took on the challenge by enduring the cross and defeating the enemy. I accept the responsibility of presenting my body a living sacrifice. Thank you Lord for getting my attention and showing me the enemy that attempts to devour me. Holy Spirit, thank you for revealing to me that I can pray for endurance when I'm tempted to lose hope. I boldly confess that that the eyes of my heart has been enlightened in order to the know the hope of His calling. Amen. *(Hebrews 12:1-2; Romans 12:1; 1 Peter 5:18; Jonah 2:7; Ephesians 1:18)*

MEDITATION

Psalm 57:7 (KJV) - My heart is fixed, O God, my heart is fixed: I will sing and give praise.

Psalm 112:7 (KJV) - He shall not be afraid of evil tidings: his heart is fixed, trusting in the Lord.

Philippians 3:13-15 (KJV) - Brethren, I count not myself to have apprehended: but this one thing I do, forgetting those things which are behind, and reaching forth unto those things which are before, I press toward the mark for the prize of the high calling of God in Christ Jesus. Let us therefore, as many as be perfect, be thus minded: and if in anything ye be otherwise minded, God shall reveal even this unto you.

Hebrews 3:1 (NIV) - Therefore, holy brothers and sisters, who share in the heavenly calling, fix your thoughts on Jesus, whom we acknowledge as our apostle and high priest.

APPLICATION

How often do you find yourself overwhelmed by life's challenges and stuck in a non-productive repetitive routine? Losing focus has the potential of causing you to neglect the basic principles of Christian living. This happens when you become preoccupied with mundane things.

Keep in mind that what you consider to be an additive may be a stronghold that could destroy your home, marriage, finances, career, ministry, and ultimately your life.

A divided and unfocused mind is an open door for chaos. To avoid this, adjust the way you think.

Consider your contribution and stop blaming others for your lack of progress. Submit your mind to Christ and dismantle all forms of ungodliness that has taken over your mind. It's imperative that you have determination to operate with a Kingdom mindset.

2 Corinthians 5:17: Therefore if any man be in Christ, he is a new creature: old things are passed away; behold, all things are become new.

Journal of Daily Reflections

Day 19
Pray

PRAYER

Dear God, I come to you with confidence knowing that you incline your ear when I pray according to your will. Because of this, I can ask what you've put in my heart. Oh Lord, my God, I will seek you daily for strength. It's my prayer that you hear the cry of your servant, *(say your name).* You promised to turn your ear toward me and heal the land if I humble myself in prayer, seek your face, and turn from sinful ways. I come to you absent of worry and fear. I have confidence that I can talk to you about everything concerning life, including my family and my ministry. Thank you for being my help! In Jesus Name, Amen. *(1 John 5:14-15; 1 Chronicles 16:11; 2 Chronicles 7:14; Philippians 4:6)*

MEDITATION

Ephesians 6:18 (KJV) - Praying always with all prayer and supplication in the Spirit, and watching thereunto with all perseverance and supplication for all saints.

Jeremiah 29:12 (KJV) - Then shall ye call upon me, and ye shall go and pray unto me, and I will hearken unto you.

Job 22:27 (KJV) - Thou shalt make thy prayer unto him, and he shall hear thee, and thou shalt pay thy vows.

Mark 11:24 (KJV) - Therefore I say unto you, What things soever ye desire, when ye pray, believe that ye receive them, and ye shall have them.

APPLICATION

Prayer is an essential part of our daily walk with the Lord. It should be a part of our daily regiment for supernatural growth, strength, and balance. We need prayer like we need Vitamin D in order to stay strong.

Prayer guides the labor pains as you travail just before giving birth to the God promise. Your victory is birthed through prayer. Answers are given through prayer.

Prayer is how we communicate with God. Prayer helps to bring us in alignment with the will of God for our life. Never cease to pray because help is on the way.

Psalm 30:5: Weeping may endure for a night, but joy cometh in the morning.

Journal of Daily Reflections

Day 20
For Better or Worse

PRAYER

God you are my strength. Thank you for making a way for me while in the desert place. I stand victorious through Christ my Lord. I refuse to be shaken by trails that has taken place in my life in the past few years. I am firmly convinced that you are holding me up with your mighty hand. Lord, I declare that even when trails come my way, my faith will produce perseverance. I put my trust in you, refusing to give up or give in. I declare a better tomorrow than what's happening today. Your plans for my life are not played out in one scene. Therefore, I am confident that better is coming and that everything happening today is working for the good of tomorrow. I shall not be moved. In Jesus Name, Amen *(Isaiah 54:17; Isaiah 43:19; James 1:3; Romans :28)*

MEDITATION

Proverbs 16:3 (NLT) - Commit your actions to the LORD, and your plans will succeed.

Psalm 37:5 (NLT) - Commit everything you do to the LORD. Trust him, and he will help you.

Galatians 6:9 (NLT) - So let's not get tired of doing what is good. At just the right time we will reap a harvest of blessing if we don't give up.

Numbers 23:19 (NLT) - God is not a man, so he does not lie. He is not human, so he does not change his mind. Has he ever spoken and failed to act? Has he ever promised and not carried it through?

APPLICATION

Commitment has almost become a thing of the past. When trouble hits, many run away from God instead of to God.

Vows exchanged during a wedding ceremony challenges the couple to take serious the covenant relationship. This relationship should not be entered into lightly but with much consideration and commitment to remain during the good and bad times.

Commitment is demonstrating our devotion and obedience to God. We have to keep a "must" in our spirit. Must is defined as being "bound to by an imperative requirement".

Ask yourself, "Am I a covenant breaker or covenant keeper? Am I committed to the vow I made to God? Do I have what it takes to stay in the race?"

The enemy desires nothing more but for you to curse God and die. He approaches at the weakest times to entice and distract you with things that appear to look better than what God has blessed you with. Remember, "The blessing of the LORD brings wealth, without painful toil for it" - Proverbs 10:22 (NIV).

Regardless of how bad the situation becomes, don't stop, don't quit, but remain committed to righteousness. Let your confession be, "for better or for worse".

Journal of Daily Reflections

I'm a Survivor

PRAYER

My Father God, thank you for understanding the tears I cry and not leaving me to fight for myself. You never abandoned me even when I was at a place of despair. What intended to destroy me, only strengthened me.. Thank you for calling me forth when others counted me out. Thank you for going to battle for me. What an experience to watch you bring deliverance in my life. I will always have praises of thanksgiving in my mouth for you, oh Lord. I will share with others all that you have done for me and we will rejoice together. Amen *(2 Corinthians 4:9; Psalm 34:1,3)*

MEDIATION

Deuteronomy 20:4 (NIV) - For the LORD your God is the one who goes with you to fight for you against your enemies to give you victory.

1 Corinthians 10:13 (NIV) - No temptation has overtaken you except what is common to mankind. And God is faithful; he will not let you be tempted beyond what you can bear. But when you are tempted, he will also provide a way out so that you can endure it.

1 Corinthians 15:57 (NIV) - But thanks be to God! He gives us the victory through our Lord Jesus Christ.

APPLICATION

As I prepared this devotion, I thought about the many battles God brought me through. Reflecting on these moments provoke the question, "how did I make it through that?" The answer is wrapped in the words of this hymn:

> **"He (*God*) touched me!** Shackled by a heavy burden, 'neath a load of guilt and shame. Then the hand of Jesus touched me, And now I am no longer the same."

I can never imagine my life without Christ. I've experienced being homeless, exposure to abuse, anxiety attacks, and grave persecution. Prayer, praise, and worship has kept me in a place of victory and prevented me from taking ownership of traumatic life experiences. God did not allow me to embrace the mentality of a victim, but proved that I am victorious.

Seeking wise counsel and constantly declaring the Word of God over my life has landed me in a place of unrestricted peace. I've finally come to realize the depth of my struggle symbolizes the height of my victory!

We all have endured various crisis and traumatic situations that only God could bring us through. Thank God that you are alive to tell your story, having victory over it all. Finish strong!

Ephesians 6:11 (NLT) - Put on all of God's armor so that you will be able to stand firm against all strategies of the devil.

Hallelujah!

Journal of Daily Reflections

CONCLUSION

Daily mediation in the Word of God coupled with prayer guarantees great success. **Joshua 1:8**, "Keep this Book of the Law always on your lips; meditate on it day and night, so that you may be careful to do everything written in it. Then you will be prosperous and successful" - (NIV).

I wrote this book with hopes that after 21 days of prayer, mediation, and application you will be encouraged to stand firm on the promises of God. Push pass all the tricks of the enemy whose purpose is to leave you without hope.

There will be moments in your life that yield strong attacks, but know that we serve a God who is greater than any problem. Remember, The Holy Spirit (paraclete - the One who walks along side to help) will enable you to arrive at your intended destination, at the appointed time, fulfilling your intended purpose *(refer to Day #17)*.

I am confident that the warrior in you will continue to slay spiritual giants. Continue to do this through prayer, meditation, and application.

Final Moment of Reflections

_____

_____

_____

_____

_____

_____

_____

_____

_____

_____

_____

_____

_____

_____

_____

_____

_____

_____

_____

_____

_____

_____

_____

_____

Final Moment of Reflections